Introduction

Imagine we disassemble a system and put its parts, components into a segment one by one, as shown schematically here:

Then we fold this segment into a square:

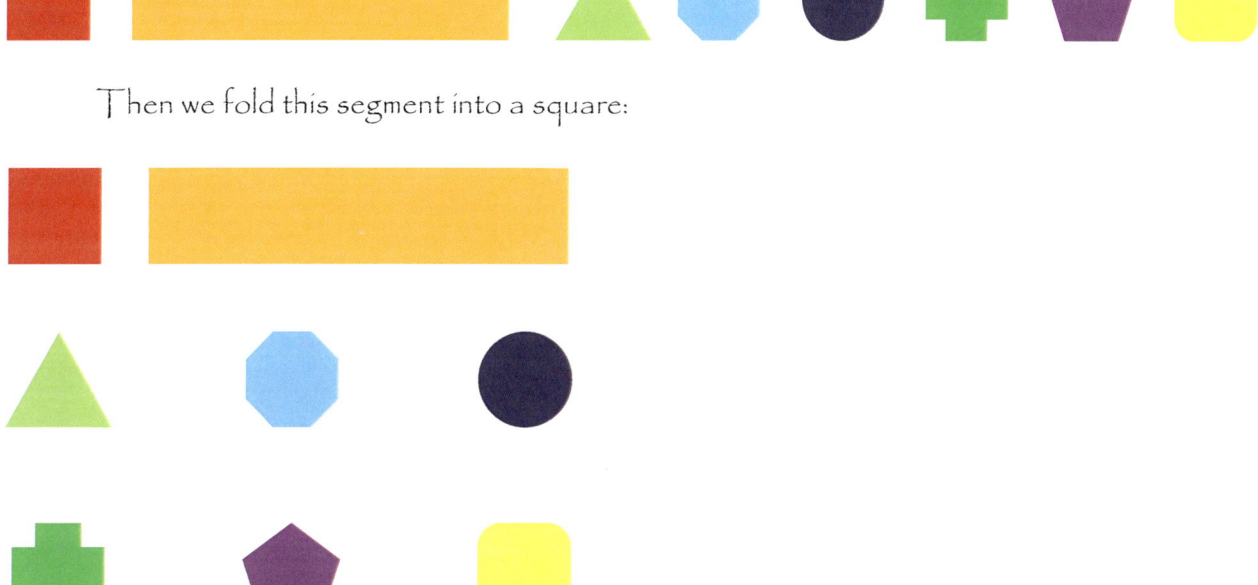

What we get is an example of a component list landscape. The same procedure can be done with a computer program assembled in linear memory from various software components called DLLs (dynamic linked libraries). Memory space, interpreted as a picture, shows characteristic patterns of components and memory region boundaries, known as the DLL list landscape.

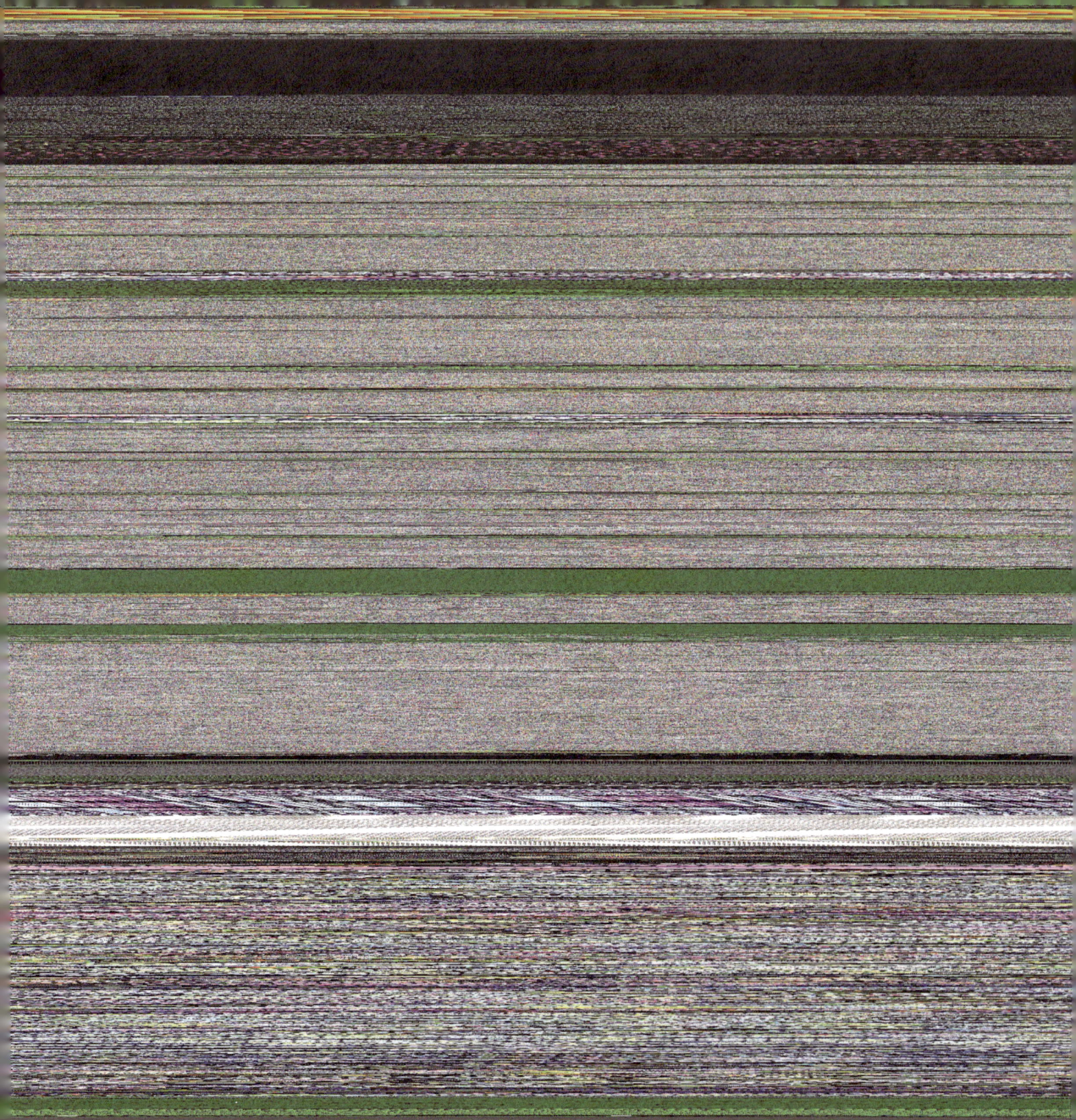

00400000	00438000	SystemDump	Tue Jan 23	2007
5ad70000	5ada8000	uxtheme	Wed Aug 04	2004
73000000	73026000	WINSPOOL	Wed Aug 04	2004
74720000	7476b000	MSCTF	Wed Aug 04	2004
77120000	771ac000	OLEAUT32	Wed Aug 04	2004
77200000				06 2006
772d0000				04 2004
773d0000				04 2004
77400000				17 2008
774e0000				04 2004
77c10000				04 2004
77d40000				04 2004
77dd0000				04 2004
77e70000				12 2005
77f10000	77f56000	GDI32	Wed Aug 04	2004
77f60000	77fd6000	SHLWAPI	Wed Aug 04	2004
7c800000	7c8f4000	kernel32	Wed Aug 04	2004
7c900000	7c9b0000	ntdll	Wed Aug 04	2004
7c9c0000	7d1d4000	SHELL32	Wed Aug 04	2004

DLL List Landscape

The Art from Computer Memory Space

Dmitry Vostokov

OpenTask

Published by OpenTask, Republic of Ireland

Copyright © 2008 by Dmitry Vostokov

All rights reserved. No part of this book may be reproduced, stored in a retrieval system, or transmitted, in any form or by any means, without the prior written permission of the publisher.

You must not circulate this book in any other binding or cover, and you must impose the same condition on any acquirer.

Microsoft and Windows are registered trademarks of Microsoft Corporation. Citrix, XenApp, and Presentation Server are registered trademarks of Citrix Systems. Other product and company names mentioned in this book may be trademarks of their owners.

OpenTask books are available through booksellers and distributors worldwide. For further information or comments, send requests to press@opentask.com.

A CIP catalogue record for this book is available from the British Library.

ISBN-13: 978-1-912636-84-6 (Paperback)

Revised second printing, 2025

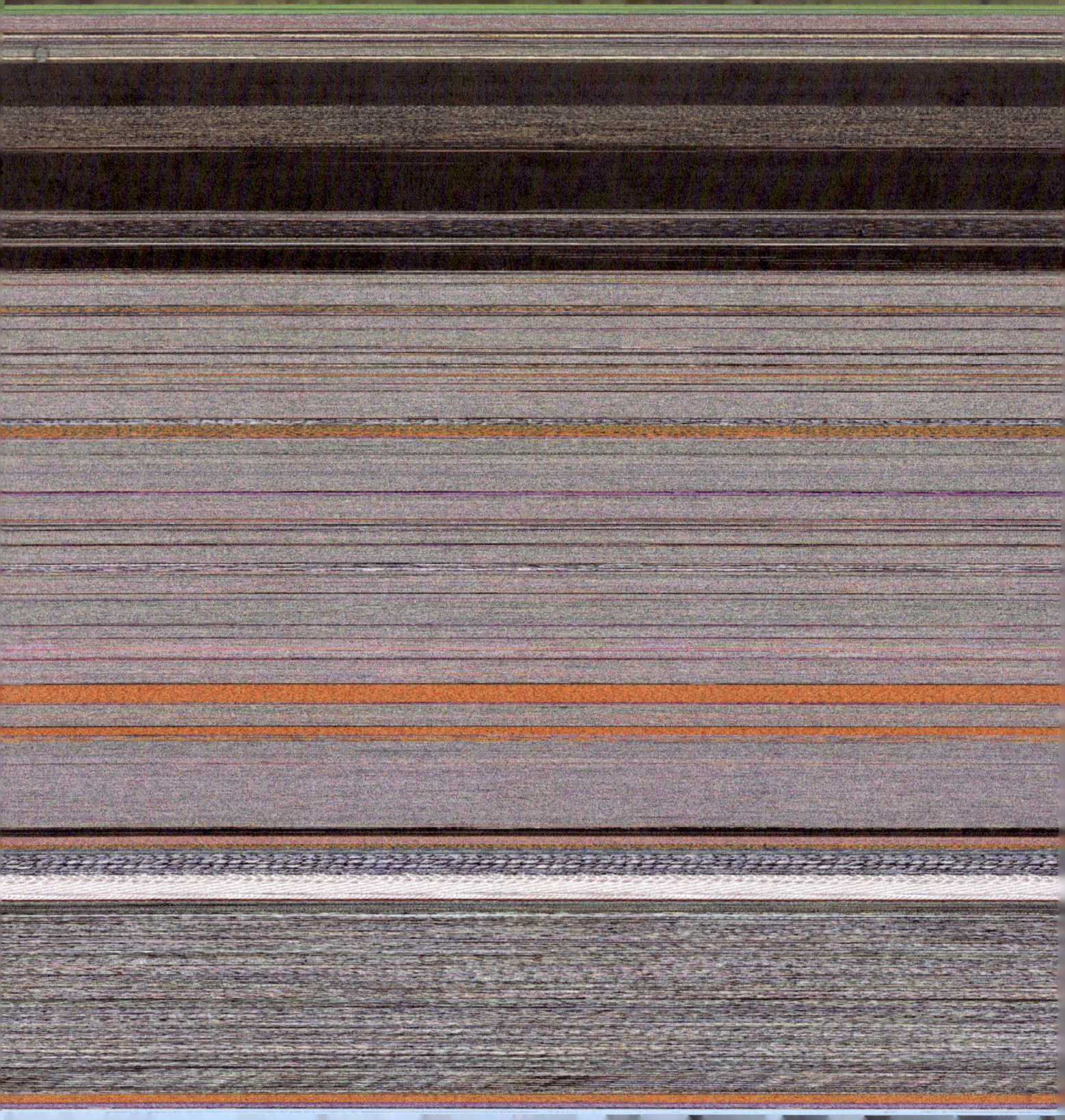

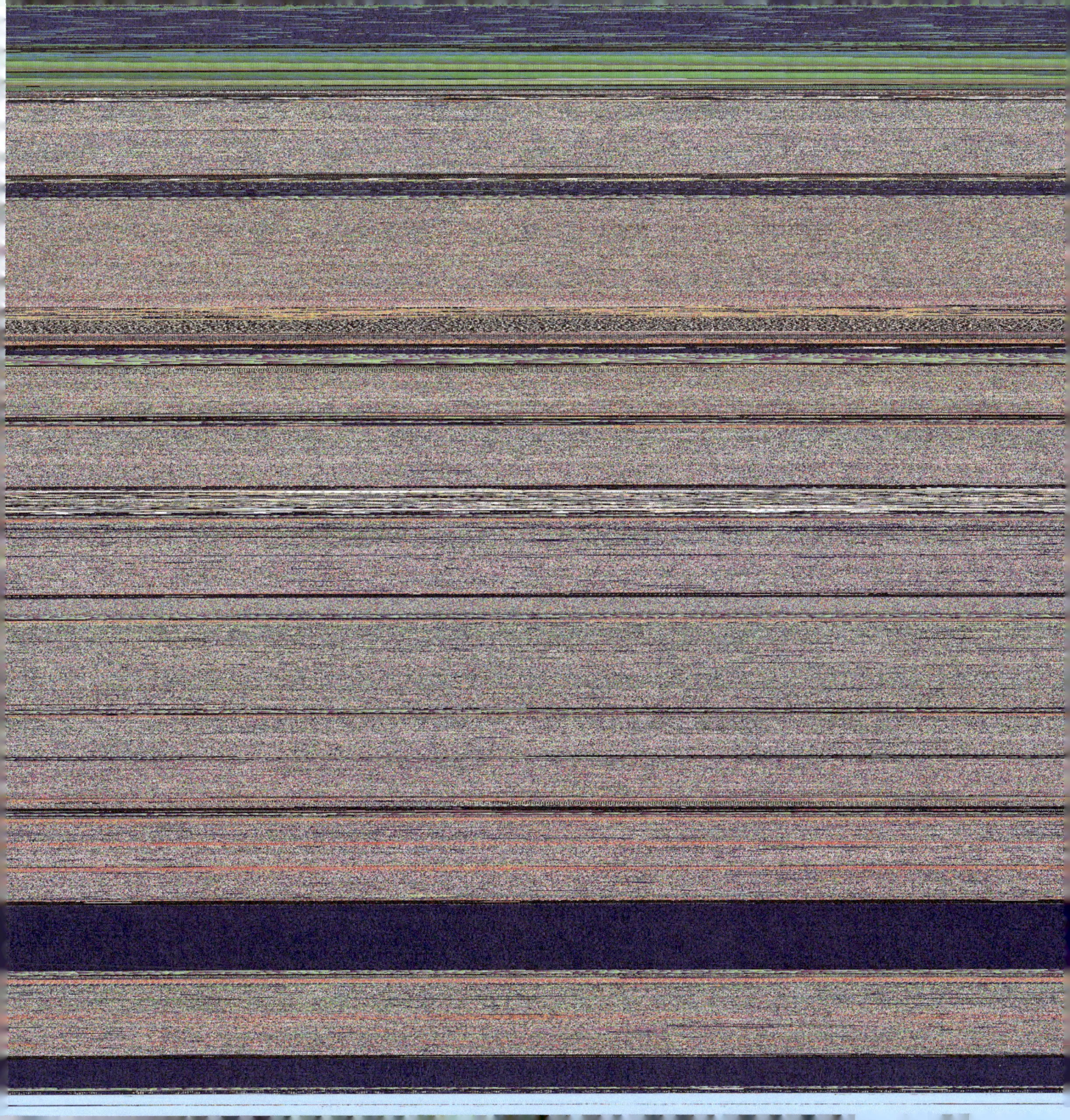

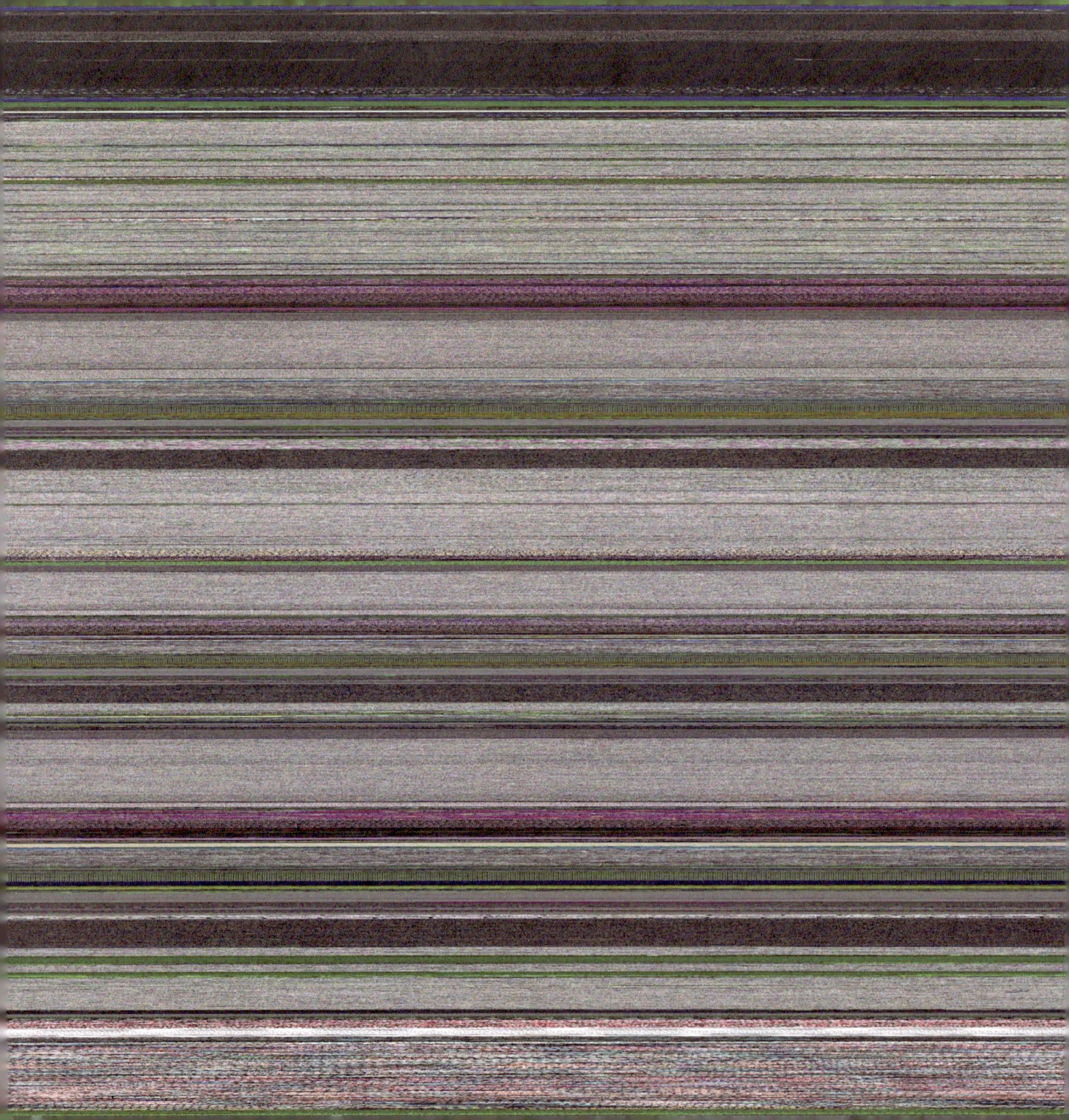

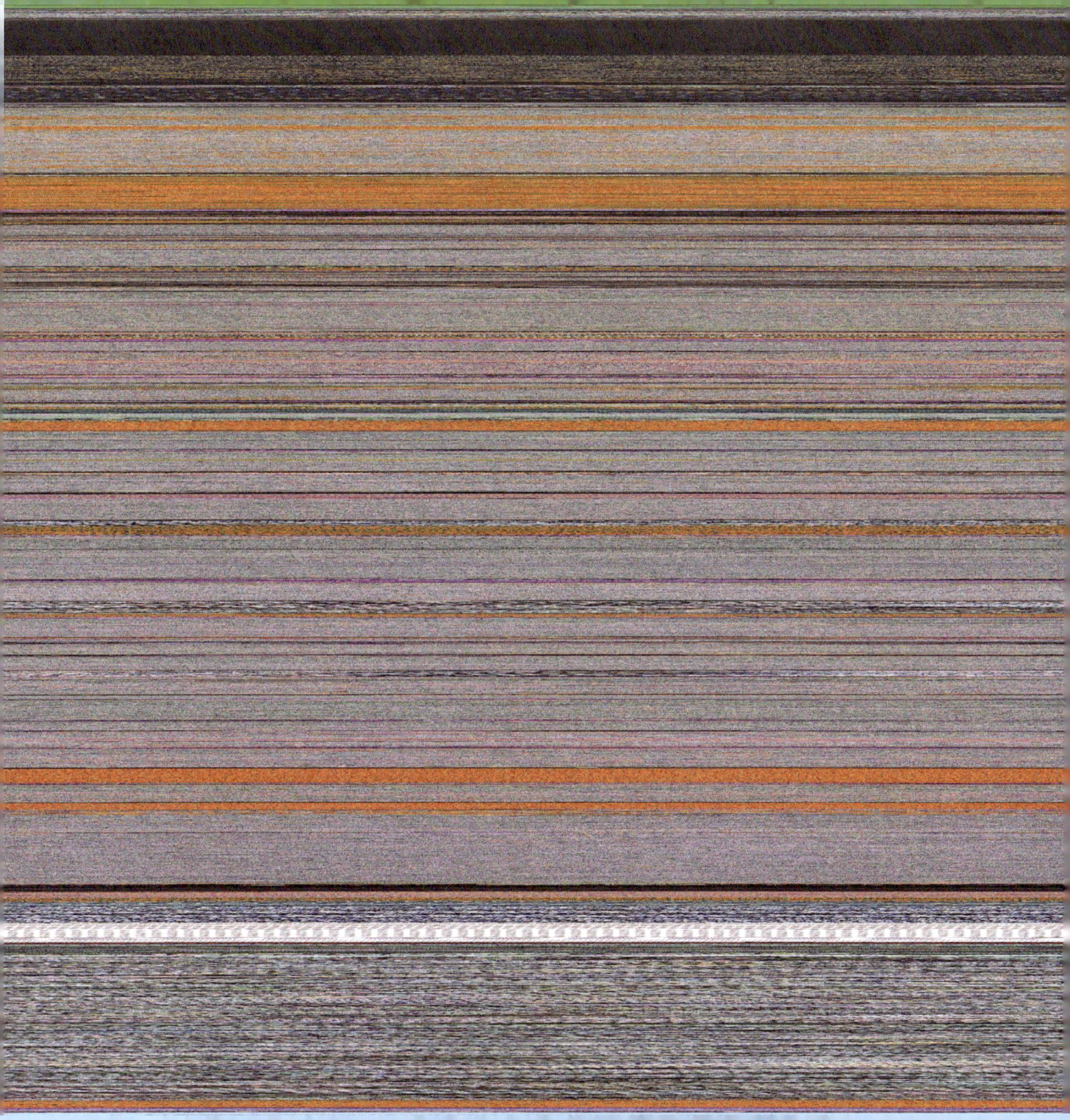

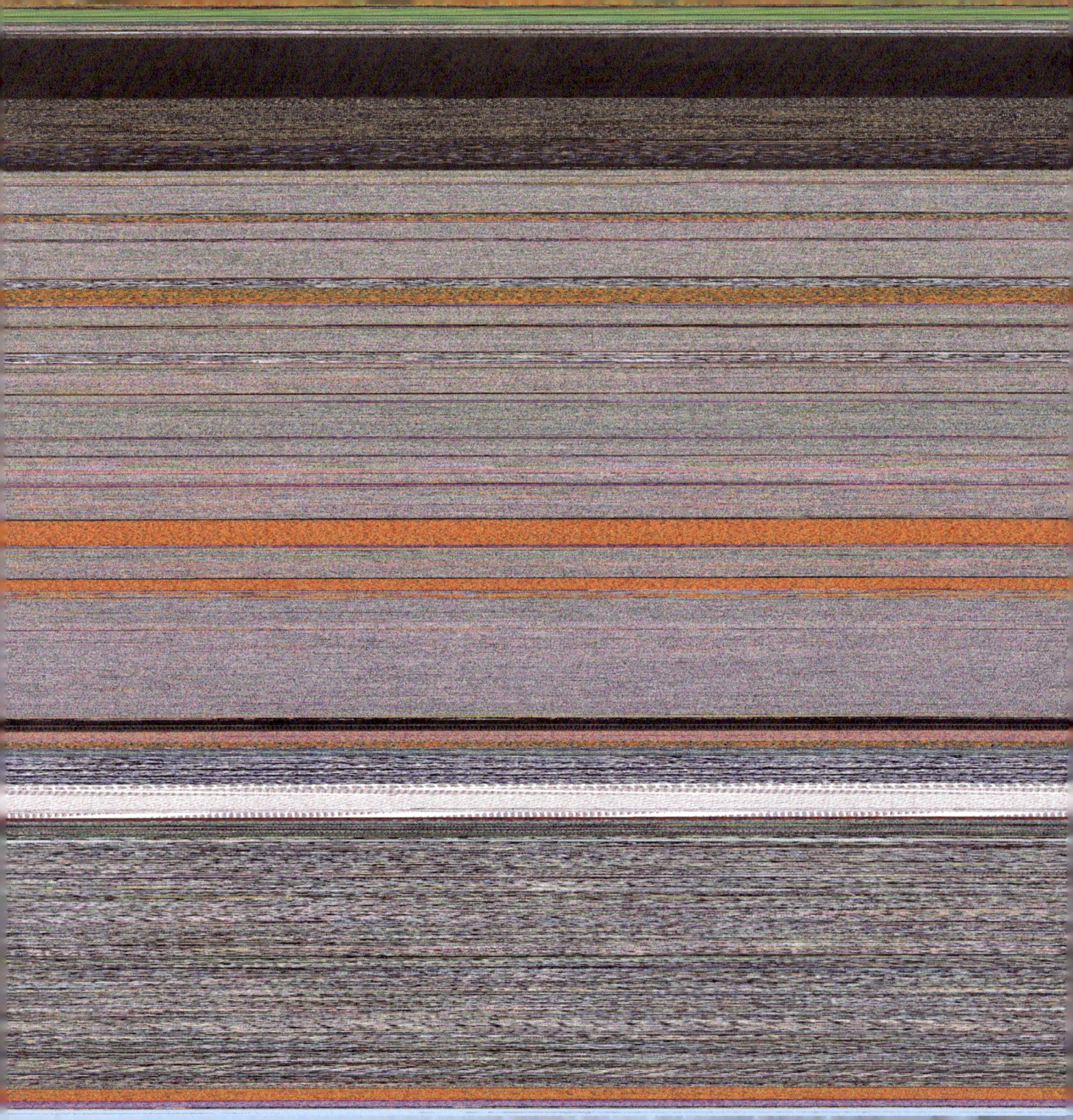

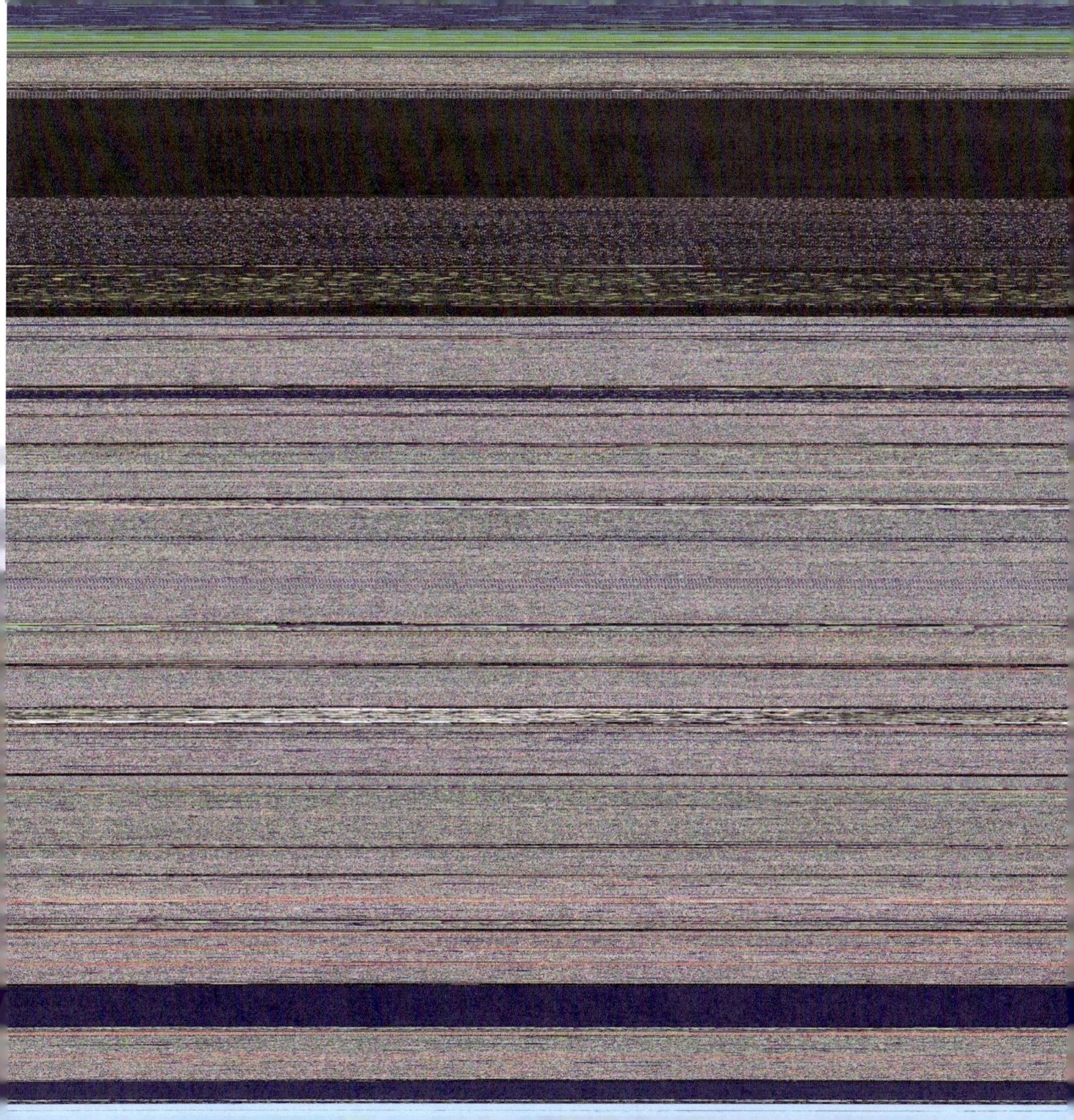

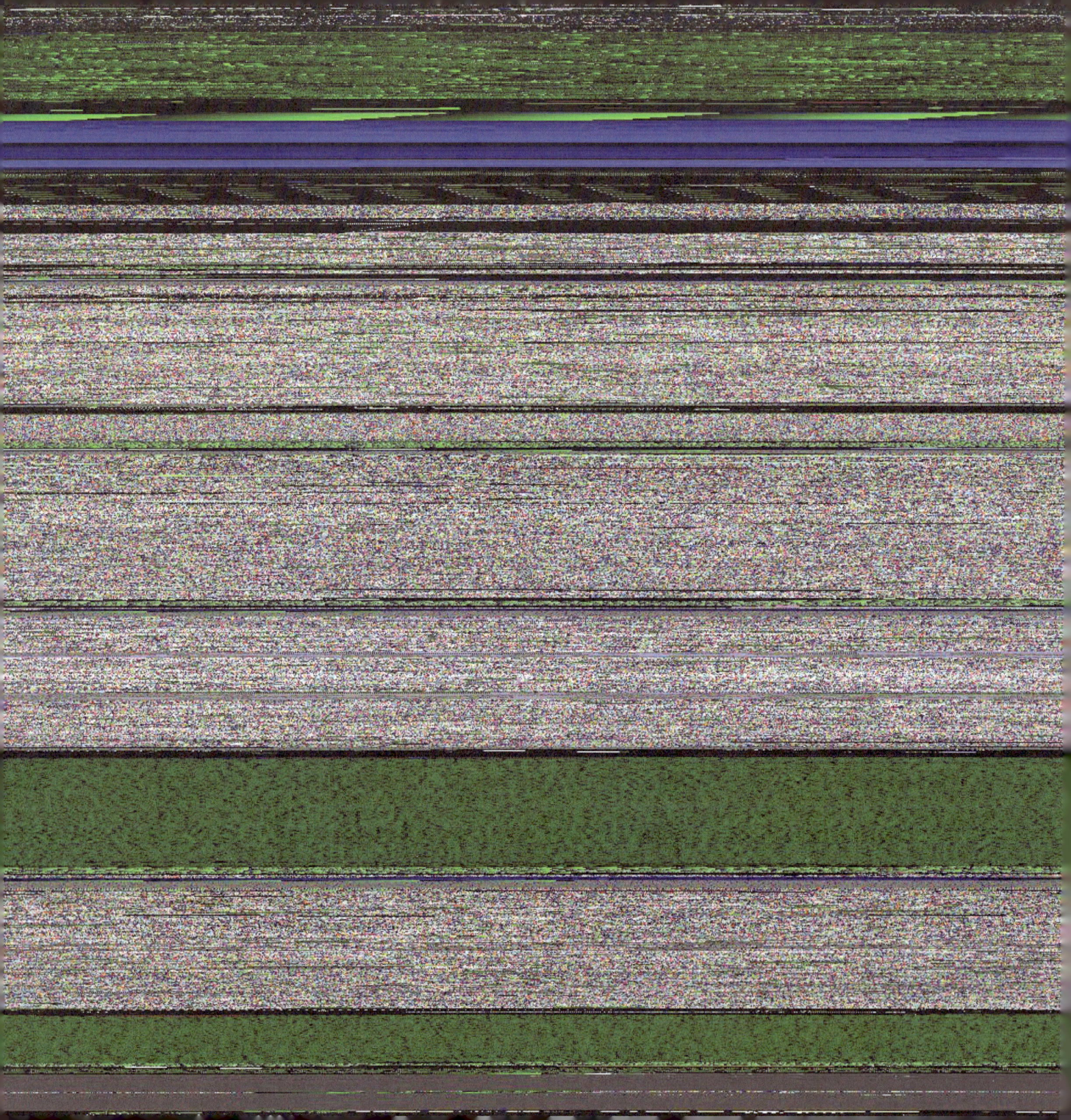

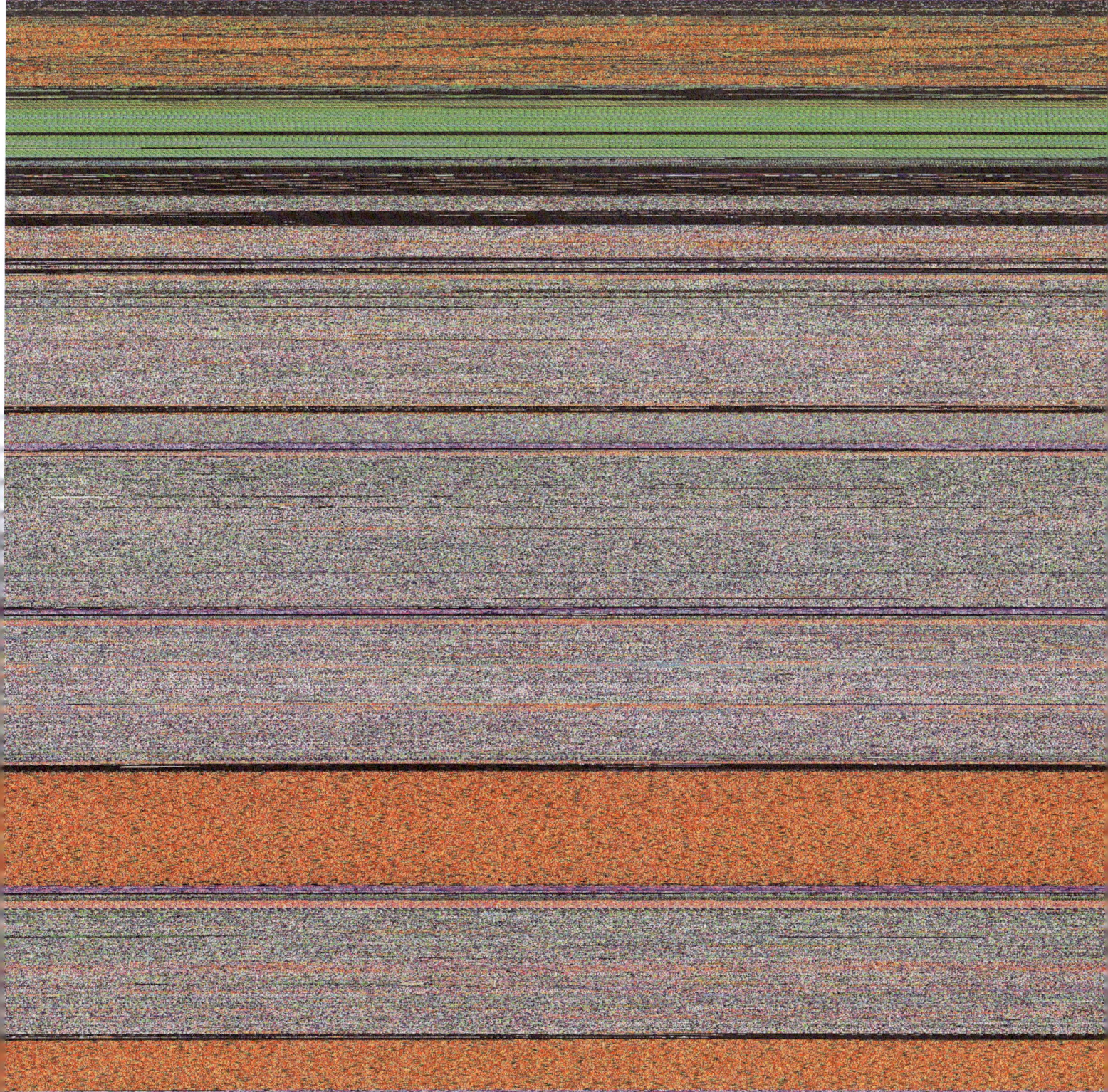

Art Recipe

Microsoft user mode process dumper, userdump.exe, was used to save a memory dump of the following free Citrix XenApp and Presentation Server tools:

SystemDump, JetTest, DSView, TestDefaultDebugger.NET, IcaFileCreator, WindowHistory, MessageHistory, CtxHideEx32, PDBFinder.

The Dump2Picture tool from DumpAnalysis.org was then used to convert memory dumps into corresponding bitmap images with 32-bit and 16-bit color depths. After that, bitmaps were saved as JPEG images, which you see in this book.

One of the process images is from the DumpAnalysis.org project called EasyDbg, and the last two images are generated from the Dump2Picture process itself (self-portraits with 32-bit and 16-bit color depths).

www.ingramcontent.com/pod-product-compliance
Lightning Source LLC
Chambersburg PA
CBRC100912220526
45473CB00011B/2871